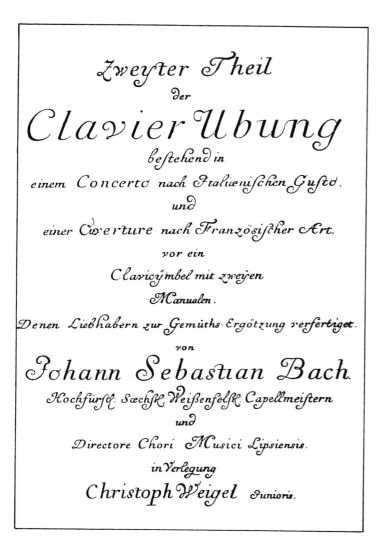

Title page and page 1 of the first edition of the *Clavierübung*, Part Two, with corrections in Bach's own hand.
Reproduced by courtesy of the Trustees of the British Museum.

ORIGIN

The *Italian Concerto* was first published in 1735 as a part of the second volume of the *Clavierübung*, which also contained the *French Overture (Partita in B Minor)*. The title page of the first edition, reproduced above, is translated as follows:

Second part of Keyboard Practice, consisting of a Concerto after the Italian taste and an Overture in the French style for a harpsichord with two manuals. Composed for music lovers for the pleasure of their minds, by Johann Sebastian Bach, chapel master of the Court of Saxe-Weisenfels, and director of the Leipzig Musical Choir. Published by Christoph Weigel, Junior.

Since no autograph of the *Italian Concerto* is known to exist, the first edition of *Clavierübung II* is the most important source. Microfilms of the following copies were used in preparing the present edition:

1. A copy from the Hirsch collection of the British Museum, catalog number III.38.

2. A copy with numerous corrections in J.S. Bach's own hand, British Museum catalog number K.8.g.7.

3. A copy of the 2nd printing of the first edition, with corrections made on the engraved plates, British Museum catalog number K.8.g.21.

Cover art: Landscape with Roman ruins, *1740*
by Giovanni Antonio Canaletto (1697–1768)
Accademia, Venice, Italy
Cameraphoto/Art Resource, New York

Alfred Music Publishing Co., Inc.
P.O. Box 10003
Van Nuys, CA 91410-0003
alfred.com

Book Alone:
ISBN-10: 0-7390-1731-4
ISBN-13: 978-0-7390-1731-9

Book & CD:
ISBN-10: 0-7390-7755-4
ISBN-13: 978-0-7390-7755-9

As an additional reference:

An 18th-century manuscript from the Hartung legacy (Bach Mus. Ms. P215) in the hand of Johann Christoph Ritter. A microfilm of this manuscript was kindly furnished by the Staatsbibliothek (Preussischer Kulturbesitz), Berlin, Musikabteilung.

The term *concerto* has its origin in the Latin *concertare*, "to strive together." It was first applied to compositions in which several instruments were merely combined "in concert." Around the end of the 17th century, many Italian composers, notably Corelli, Torelli and Vivaldi, were using the title for compositions in which a small group of solo instruments (usually strings) was heard in alternation and in combination with a larger body of instruments. These concertos, known as *concerti grossi*, were generally in three contrasting movements. The most famous of the *concerti grossi* are J.S. Bach's six *Brandenburg Concertos*.

The following comments were written in 1739 by Johann Adolph Scheibe, a famous German theorist and critic:

Concertos are also written for a single instrument alone, without any accompaniment by others, especially clavier concertos and lute concertos. In such pieces the basic structure remains the same as in concertos for many instruments.

In the same article, Scheibe specifically mentions the *Italian Concerto:*

Pre-eminent among published musical works is a clavier concerto, the composer of which is the famous Bach of Leipzig, and which is in the key of F major. Since the piece is arranged in the best possible fashion for such a work, I believe it should doubtless become familiar to all great composers and experienced clavier players, as well as the amateurs of the clavier and music in general. Who is there who will not at once admit that this clavier concerto is to be regarded as the perfect model of the well-designed solo concerto?

ORNAMENTATION

THE EXPLICATION

The following table of ornaments from the *Clavier-Büchlein vor Wilhelm Friedemann Bach* is the only such table known to have been prepared by J.S. Bach.

Reproduced by courtesy of the Yale University School of Music.

1. THE TRILL $\mathcal{w}$ $\mathcal{ww}$ tr

In Bach's music these three symbols are used interchangeably. Each may indicate a long or a short trill.

This fact is verified in the corrections made by Bach himself in a copy of the first edition of the *Italian Concerto.* In several places in the first movement (for example, in the 34th measure), Bach expressed the trill as a line only slightly waved. The engraver drew these marks as nearly straight lines. Bach corrected these errors in his own copy (No. 2 of the sources listed on page 1) by writing the symbol *tr* over the incorrectly engraved ornaments. In the second printing of the edition the lines were made more wavy. These ornaments are trills whether written $\mathcal{w}$ or *tr* . In his *Essay on the True Art of Playing Keyboard Instruments,* C.P.E. Bach makes it very clear that the symbols $\mathcal{w}$, $\mathcal{ww}$ and *tr* are synonymous.

It is not possible to overemphasize the fact that *all* trills begin on the *upper auxiliary*. In C.P.E. Bach's *Essay* he says of the trill, "it always begins on the tone above the principal note." This fact is borne out in Bach's own realization of the trill, the first example in the *Explication,* reproduced on page 2.

In the *Explication,* the manner of execution of the trill is illustrated only for the trill on a quarter note. This can only serve to give the general configuration, since the number of repercussions in a trill depends upon the tempo as well as the time-value of the note upon which it occurs.

The trill often comes to rest on the principal note but sometimes may continue for the entire value of the note.

In the 46th measure of the first movement of the *Italian Concerto,* on page 10, the trill occurs on a sixteenth note. Because of the tempo of the movement it is impractical to stop the trill on the principal note before proceeding:

written: played:

The trills on sixteenth notes in the second movement, however, may be brought to rest on the principal notes with good effect, because of the slower tempo of the movement. This example is found in the 7th measure, on page 18:

written: played:

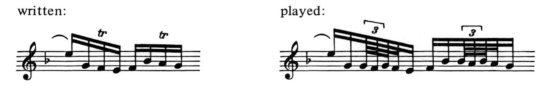

In the 34th measure of the first movement, on page 10, the trill occurs on an eighth note. The following realizations are possible:

written: played:

Trills on long notes need not be precisely measured; that is, they need not have a certain number of repercussions per beat. They may begin slowly, lingering a bit on the first note, then gradually increasing in speed and continuing for the entire value of the note, or coming to rest on the principal note.

2. THE TRILL WITH TERMINATION

The termination consists of two notes connected to the trill, performed at the same speed as the trill.

The trill requires a minimum of four notes, and the termination consists of two notes:

The trill with termination may be indicated by the symbols ⟨symbol⟩ or ⟨symbol⟩ (these symbols are not used in the *Italian Concerto*) or the termination may be written out in notes following the trill.

According to the instructions of C.P.E. Bach, a termination may often be added to a trill, even when it is not indicated in the music. Short or long trills ascending stepwise to the following note are usually most effective with a termination. An example of this is found in the *Italian Concerto* in measure 106 of the third movement, on page 27.

written:

played:

3. THE MORDENT ⟨symbol⟩

The word *mordent* comes from the Latin *mordere,* meaning "to bite." This describes the incisive quality of the mordent, which is played very quickly.

The function of the mordent, according to C.P.E. Bach's *Essay*, is "to connect notes, fill them out, and make them brilliant."

The only mordents used in the *Italian Concerto* occur in the second movement. Some artists play these mordents very slowly, and with good effect, but the editors of the present edition can find no precedent for this manner of performance.

In reference to mordents used to fill out long notes, C.P.E. Bach recommends the use of the long mordent; that is, a mordent with additional repercussions. Such a mordent is usually indicated by the symbol ⟨symbol⟩ or ⟨symbol⟩ . He states that "it is customary to play the long mordent only on long notes and the short mordent on short notes," but he adds that "the symbol for the long mordent is often found over quarters and eighths, depending on the tempo, and that of the short mordent over notes of all values and lengths."

In the second movement of the *Italian Concerto*, in measure 4 on page 18, Bach has clearly indicated a short mordent.

written:

played:

If the ornament is played as a long mordent, as some prefer, the following realizations are possible:

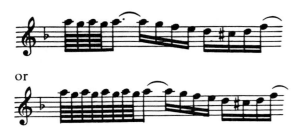

or

According to C.P.E. Bach, the long mordent must stop on the principal note. "A small fraction of the original length must remain free of decoration," he writes, "because the most perfectly introduced mordent sounds miserable when, like the trill, it speeds directly into the following tone."

4. THE ASCENDING TRILL

This ornament is also called the *trill with prefix from below*. The configuration of this trill is similar to the shape of the written ornament.

The prefix consists of two notes; the trill requires a minimum of four notes:

Prefix   Trill

In the *Italian Concerto* the ornament occurs in measures 112, 116, 135 and 137 of the first movement. It also appears in the second movement in measures 26, 44 and 48, each time followed by a written termination. The notes of the termination are played at the same speed as the notes of the trill, regardless of the values of the written notes. The following example is from the second movement, measure 26, page 20:

written:

played:

5. THE DESCENDING TRILL

This ornament is also called the *trill with prefix from above*. Its configuration is similar to the shape of the written ornament.

The prefix consists of four notes; the trill requires a minimum of four notes:

Prefix   Trill

In the *Italian Concerto* this ornament occurs in the second movement, in the 17th measure, on page 19.

written:

played:

6. THE APPOGGIATURA

The *Italian Concerto* contains many appoggiaturas, most of which are written out in regular notes; thus the time values are clearly indicated. Only two are indicated by small notes. These are in the second movement, on page 18, in measures 8 and 9.

The general rules for appoggiaturas, set forth by the writers of the period, state:

  a. The appoggiatura is played *on the beat*.

  b. The appoggiatura takes *half* the time value from the following note, except when that note is a dotted note, in which case it takes *two-thirds* of the time value.

The second of the above rules cannot be applied to the appoggiatura in the 8th measure (page 18), written:

If the appoggiatura is given the value of a quarter note, consecutive fifths result with the upper tone of the left hand part:

If the appoggiatura is further lengthened and given the value of a dotted quarter note, consecutive octaves result with the lower tone of the left hand part.

For the reasons stated above, most artists perform the ornament in one of the following ways:

The fact that the appoggiatura is written as a small eighth note would seem to indicate that it should be played as an eighth note. C.P.E. Bach endorsed the practice of showing the duration of the small note by using notation corresponding to the true length of the note, but this system was seldom used by J.S. Bach, if at all.

To the editors of the present edition, this appoggiatura is most satisfactorily performed as a sixteenth note. This agrees with the appoggiaturas written out in large notes in subsequent measures (see measures 11, 16, 17, 19, etc.).

The appoggiatura in measure 9 should be performed at the same value as the one in measure 8.

ARTICULATION AND PHRASING

In his biography of J.S. Bach, Forkel describes the touch Bach cultivated in his students as being such that "tones are neither disjoined from each other nor blended together." To this, he adds, "the touch is, therefore, as C. Ph. E. Bach says, neither too long nor too short, but just what it ought to be." He mentions that Bach played with curved fingers, with the tips perpendicular to the keys, and with a very quiet hand and arm. The result, he said, was "the highest degree of clearness in the expression of individual notes."

These comments, taken from information given Forkel by Bach's sons, may be applied to Bach's music only in a general way. Bach certainly stressed legato playing, as is evidenced by his references to the importance of developing the "cantabile" style of playing in his foreword to the *Inventions & Sinfonias.* C.P.E. Bach points out that the legato style is appropriate in slower movements and the detached style in faster ones. Such an observation can be applied to the *Italian Concerto.* The basic style of the first and third movements should be detached, and that of the second movement, legato.

The slurs in dark print in the present edition are Bach's own indications, taken from the original edition. Those in lighter print are added by the editors. They may be observed or disregarded at the discretion of the individual.

One important convention of the period is often overlooked. In his *Essay,* C.P.E. Bach states that the slurred notes of broken chords are held in the manner shown in the following example:

written:

played:

This convention may be applied to several measures of the *Italian Concerto*; for example, in the broken chords in measures 15 through 20, on page 9.

DYNAMICS

The *Italian Concerto* is one of the very few of Bach's works that contain the authentic indications *forte* and *piano*. These words are written out in full; the abbreviations f and p were not used in Bach's time.

These contrasting dynamic effects were possible on the two-manual harpsichord, for which the work was composed. The *forte* sections were to be played on a manual employing two strings for each key, the 8' and 4' registers, which sounded the written note and the tone an octave higher. The *piano* sections were played on the other manual, which sounded only one string per key, usually a softer, single 8' tone, sounding only the written pitch.

On some instruments the manuals could be coupled so that the sound of the softer manual was added to the louder one (but not vice versa) for additional dynamic contrast. These changes in dynamics make possible the imitation of the *concerto grosso* style and justify the title of the work.

In playing this work on the piano it is important to bear in mind that the *forte–piano* effect possible on the harpsichord is by no means the same as that produced by the piano. The performer must use good taste and judgment in contrasting those parts in which both staffs are marked *forte,* representing the orchestral *tutti,* with those in which both staffs are marked *piano,* representing the *concertino* sections of the work. The nuances within such sections must not be so extreme as to obliterate the basic architecture of the piece. The parts marked *forte* for one hand and *piano* for the other should indicate, for the pianist, a logical amount of prominence of one hand over the other throughout the section.

In the second movement Bach's only instructions are *forte* for the right hand and *piano* for the left hand, at the beginning. The upper part is written in the style of an instrumental solo, while the left provides an accompaniment in two parts. In this movement, the piano is capable of an *espressivo* style not quite possible on the harpsichord, but such an effect should not be overdone.

Continued on page 32.

ITALIAN CONCERTO

J.S. Bach, B.W.V. 971

(a) For the meaning of the *forte* and *piano* indications, see page 7. The *forte's* at the beginning do not appear in the sources but are understood. All of Bach's concerti grossi begin with the tutti.

(b) All of the original sources show the rhythm as given above. It is quite probable it was intended to be as follows:

This is identical with the rhythm in related passages found in measures 73-74 and 175-176. Most editors make this change.

10

(d) On a two-manual instrument the middle voice should be played on the softer manual by the left hand, together with the lower voice.

(e) The slurs in the first edition were carelessly drawn. See the last four measures of the facsimile on page 1.

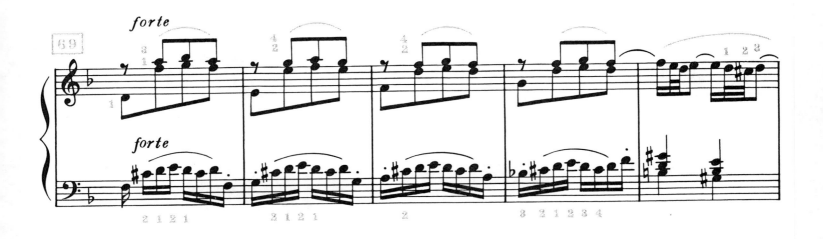

① The **pp** found here in most editions, originating with Hans von Bülow, is contrary to the basic architecture of the movement.

(g) The presence of the *piano* for the left hand part in measures 90 and 129 makes it obvious that *forte* was intended somewhere between: undoubtedly at the beginning of this measure.

(h) The original edition has C, probably an engraver's error. Our text agrees with the Hartung manuscript (P215).

(i) Bach's corrected copy of the first printing of the original edition has *tr* here and in measure 116. The trills were changed in the second printing to ∿ as in our text. It is not necessary that the trills have a prescribed number of repercussions.

(j) The first printing of the original edition has *tr* here and in measure 137. The trills were changed to ∼∼∼ in the second printing.

16

18

(a) See the discussion of this mordent, beginning on page 4.

(b) It is impossible to determine exactly which notes are included under the slurs in this movement in the original edition.

(c) The Hartung manuscript (P215) has B♮ instead of B♭.

(d) These appoggiaturas may be played as eighth notes, if preferred. See the discussion on page 5.

19

(e) Here the Peters Urtext and the Bischoff edition have a mordent, probably derived from the Hartung manuscript (P215). Bach's corrected copy definitely has *tr*. The trill may be realized as shown in our text, or in one of the following ways:

(f) The Hartung manuscript has $\text{l}\!\!\mu\!\!\sim$, a prepared trill, indicating a prolonging of the first note (the upper auxiliary) before continuing the trill.

(a) The *forte* above the treble applies to both staffs. This is indicated in the original edition by a bracket enclosing all 3 voices: The Hartung manuscript interpreted this bracket as $\{$, indicating a broken chord, and added the same sign at the beginning of the recapitulation in measure 199, where no bracket was used by Bach.

24

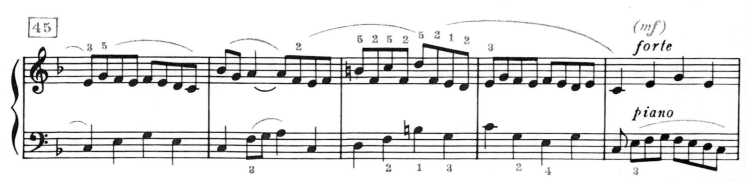

(b) The Hartung manuscript has simply *tr*.

ⓒ The Bischoff edition has ⌣⌣.

ⓓ In the first printing of the original edition a trill appears on the F♯. It was deleted in the second printing.

e) The *forte* is from the Hartung manuscript. It is omitted in the original edition, an obvious error, since *piano* is indicated above the treble staff in measure 127 and again in measure 155.

30

Continued from page 7.

TEMPOS

J.S. Bach rarely gave tempo indications for his music. Fortunately, he did indicate tempos for the 2nd and 3rd movements of the *Italian Concerto*. The 1st movement is undoubtedly intended to be played *Allegro*. Such tempo markings as *Allegro, Andante,* and *Presto* allow considerable license for the individual. The tempo may vary not only with the temperament of the performer, but with the responsiveness and tone of an individual instrument and the acoustics and resonance of a room or hall.

A survey of tempos used by various recording artists yields the following interesting range of tempos:

The 1st movement was played as slow as ♩ = 108 and as fast as ♩ = 126.

The 2nd movement was played as slow as ♪ = 54 and as fast as ♪ = 90.

The 3rd movement was played as slow as 𝅝 = 126 and as fast as 𝅝 = 152.

ACKNOWLEDGEMENTS

The editors express their appreciation to the Trustees of the British Museum for the use of microfilms of the first edition, for permission to reproduce the facsimiles used in this book, and for permission to publish the present edition. They also thank Iris and Morton Manus for their assistance in preparing the final engravings of this edition.